TOBIT DETOURS

I don't know a better way to become acquainted with an obscure apocryphal cast of characters than to read Elisabeth Mehl Greene's poetry. She breathes magic and humor into ancient texts in a style not terribly unlike Jonathan Goldstein. She can take a dry story and show us a new perspective, throwing us into the minds of unnamed female characters, demons, angels, and camels—allowing each of them their well-deserved voices. Even if you've never heard of Tobit, Greene makes his story accessible and wildly entertaining. Combining rich vocabulary with modern slang, her wry wit sings through every page. Come for the gravedigging, stay for the angel pranks.

—JOANN RENEE BOSWELL,
author of *Meta-Verse* and *Cosmic Pockets*

In *Tobit Detours*, Elisabeth Mehl Greene brings to life a little-known biblical text and infuses it with wit and verve. Greene brings her characters to vivid life and brings them into the modern world, giving them modern English to speak while depicting their essential qualities and quirks. One does not need to be a believer to find charm and wisdom herein. Enter Tobit's world as presented by Greene and savor its color and substance.

—GREGORY LUCE,
Poetry Editor, *Bourgeon*, and author of *Riffs & Improvisations*

Tobit Detours: part Punch and Judy show, part Shakespearean comedy, part Homeric journey, part Joycean play on words. This narrative in verse by Elisabeth Mehl Greene, scholar and artist, with its epic cast of characters, mystifies, teases, and delights.

—ANNE BECKER,
author of *Human Animal*

In many ways, the Book of Tobit is the quintessential work of apocrypha: it's got a plucky young hero, a murderous demon, an avenging angel, an unlikely love story, and poop-related injury. With *Tobit Detours*, Greene has taken all the appeal of the ancient story and updated it for the post-modern reader with genuine emotion, elegant style, pointed wit, and knowing winks. A pleasure to read.

—Benito Cereno,
Apocrypals podcast

TOBIT DETOURS

By Elisabeth Mehl Greene

Fernwood
PRESS

Tobit Detours

Fernwood Press
Newberg, Oregon
www.fernwoodpress.com

Printed in the United States of America

Cover and page design: Mareesa Fawver Moss
Cover based on a photo by Hasan Almasi

ISBN 978-1-59498-119-7

For Lori of the North Shore, wise in the art of adaptation.

Contents

Introduction

If Tobit is the eponymous center of the deuterocanonical/apocryphal Book of Tobit, *Tobit Detours* examines the outward spiral: departures to the peripheries of the tale, its interconnectivity with the Hebrew Bible, and the ripple effects going to and from other literature.

As my first book, *Lady Midrash*, specifically listened to women of the Hebrew Bible and New Testament, this work began by setting out to interrogate female characters surrounding Tobit and his son Tobias, from the most prominent figures such as Sarah, Anna, and Edna, extending to outward circles to include the wife of Tobit's nephew Ahiqar, a maid in Sarah's household, finally zooming out to see the hand of the Queen of Assyria altering the fates of Tobit and Sarah from the halls of power.

This retelling continues investigating, extending into the realms of the fantastic, exploring the characters of Raphael the angel and Asmodeus the demon. Both characters are shadowed in mysteries and contradictions in the original text. In a travel story where geography is pivotal, their journeys are not always logical or easily traceable on the map. Human characters Tobit and Sarah begin the tale yearning for the end of their personal sufferings, not knowing the forces of heaven and hell have their own scores to settle, leading to both tragic and humorous results.

The style of this piece is influenced by interdisciplinary art, drawing from the defiant word art of Barbara Kruger, found art clusters of Nina Katchadourian, and poet Mohja Kahf's bold juxtapositions of ancient stories with modernity. Furthermore, the poem–narrative interacts with ancient texts such as the books of Jonah and *The Odyssey*, and later works such as Shakespeare's *Hamlet* and Byron's poem, "The Destruction of Sennacherib."

What is The Book of Tobit?

The Book of Tobit is a biblical novella, believed to be written around second century BCE. The original language and provenance are debated. The Dead Sea Scrolls included fragments of Tobit in both Aramaic and Hebrew. Two major Greek translations are extant. Several factors suggest that the story might have been written by Jews in the diaspora. Tobit is not included in the Jewish canon; it is considered canon for Catholic and Orthodox churches, and apocryphal for Protestants.

Tobit Who?

The central character Tobit is a Jewish man exiled in Nineveh in Assyria, whose faith is tested by adverse circumstances. The narrative surrounds misadventures of Tobit, his son Tobias, Tobias's future wife Sarah, and their families, with the intervention of supernatural personae.

Further Reading

Naomi S. S. Jacobs, "Tobit," in *The Jewish Annotated Apocrypha*, ed. Jonathan Klawans and Lawrence M. Wills (Oxford: Oxford University Press, 2020), 149-175.

Irene Nowell, *New Collegeville Bible Commentary on Jonah, Tobit, Judith* (Collegeville: Liturgical Press, 2015), 18–56.

Malka Z. Simkovich, "Sefer Tuviah, the Book of Tobit: An Ancient Jewish Novel for Shavuot," https://www.thetorah.com/article/sefer-tuviah-the-book-of-tobit-an-ancient-jewish-novel-for-shavuot.

James C. VanderKam, *An Introduction to Early Judaism* (Grand Rapids: Eerdmans, 2001), 69–71.

Cast of Characters

HOUSE OF TOBIT

Tobit, Jewish exile living in Nineveh (modern-day Mosul, Iraq)

Anna, wife of Tobit

Tobias, son of Tobit

Ahiqar, cousin of Tobit, former accountant for the King of Assyria

HOUSE OF SARAH

Sarah, Jewish exile living in Ecbatana, Media (in western Iran)

Edna, mother of Sarah

Raguel, father of Sarah

Taxma, maidservant

Maidservants

ADDITIONAL CHARACTERS

Asmodeus, demon/jinn/spirit

Raphael, archangel, alias Azariah

Gabael, cousin of Tobit, living in Rages, Media (located in the greater Tehran area, Iran) with whom Tobit left ten talents

Nuur, Ahiqar's wife

Naqi'a Zakutú, Queen of Assyria, wife of Sennacherib

Tov, Azari, Asiel, Raphael, Ella, Eden, Hannah, Tigris, Raguel, Naphtali, Nahum, Seraphina, children of Sarah and Tobias

Sarah T. Toviah, modern scholar of ancient Near Eastern languages

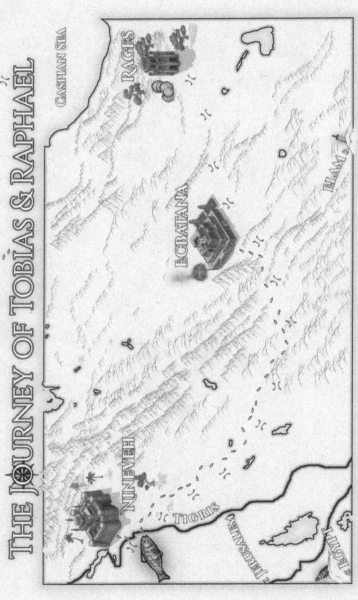

THE JOURNEY OF TOBIAS & RAPHAEL

CASPIAN SEA

RAGES

ECBATANA

ELAM

NINEVEH

TIGRIS

JERUSALEM

EGYPT

I'VE BEEN THERE MANY TIMES AND KNOW ALL OF THE WAYS ONE MIGHT ARRIVE

Part I:

CLASH OF CIRCUMSTANCE

Tobit, Jewish exile/civil disobedience activist in Nineveh, suffers a terrible accident while performing illegal burials; at the same time in Media, distant cousin Sarah is afflicted by the presence of a demon, Asmodeus, who routinely murders her consecutive grooms on their wedding nights. As Tobit and Sarah both pray for death to end their sufferings, the archangel Raphael is summoned from heaven, unbeknownst to all, including Anna, Tobit's wife, who endures his pious self-pity. Cousin Ahiqar assists Tobit's family, but two years of service exhaust his patience. Working outside the home, Anna suffers false accusations from Tobit when she brings home a bonus with her wages. And Tobit advises his son Tobias to hit the road east and collect a long-lost debt in Media.

Far from Jerusalem in the heart of the Assyrian empire,
on an unremarkable side street
of its capital city, Nineveh…

Gravedigger: Before

Night. Dark theater, yellow center spot on Tobit,
alone onstage, leaning on a spade.

TOBIT
The act of bearing witness
arc of my arm
driven shovel

Your life, cut short
minutes, days, months, decades…
vigil observed

At least by one—
valued, remembered,
recognized familiar strangers

Dirt I lift embraces your face[1]
the ground a pillow for your head
what's left of it

Comforter for your limbs
what I dig, earth delved
receives your memories

Infinite treasures
hidden, lost songs[2]
silenced scream

I hide you from the world,
from grim future,
further injury, inquiry

From dear ones who might lose faith
watching time erode by the road
what's left in shame

Choke wide-eyed prayers
spade the graves, dance
late ritual, steal from gravel

Uncover holiness
in the unclean, covering
God's work, planting the children

Closing eyelids
find extremities, matching
legs to feet, arms to hands

Lay grief to rest, again
renewed exhausted muscle
well spent

Grounded,
avenge your deaths
with my only sword:

A ploughshare

One: Tobit *After*

Day. Stage lights up on Tobit, sitting on his doorstep.

TOBIT
Obviously I walked righteously
all my days, performing charity
for kindred souls also in captivity
(under protest) based in Nineveh

Before all that, I alone
brought Jerusalem's due
while my colleagues offered
idols their barbecue

Then I'd give a second gift
of funds, third gift to the poor,
among my good deeds most obediently

Married Anna, fathered a son—
Tobias, our line of *good* continues
from Tobit and my father Tobiel,
so good I avoid foreign local foods too

With all of these good deeds
landed a sweet job with Shalmaneser,
the King, as his Agent of Purchasing

Did I mention I donate food,
contribute shelter to the poor?
And bury dead by stealth illegally?

New king Sennacherib's not a fan
of me—his army ranges every route
hunting for yours truly

So then my son young Toby
learns of a murder one cloudy night[3]
leave hot dinner for the graveyard shift
hey, no one else will do it

But like an idiot I sleep outside,
(it's summer and I smell like corpse)
and damn birds defecate in my eyes
thus I'm blind, years of doctors can't cure it

Naturally the next thing to do—
accuse breadwinner wife of stealing
and pray for a strangling

Two: Sarah

At the same time, east of the river
in Media, Sarah endured reproach
from her maidservants

For she had been given in marriage
not once or twice but to seven husbands
one after another

Sarah was widowed
each time because the demon
Asmodeus killed her bridegrooms
on their wedding night

EDNA, mother of the bride
She shreds
rosewater crushed and distilled

Sarah, my only daughter sweats
her prayers for death

MAIDSERVANTS
Miss A-Little-Nervous—we get it!
make an impression

get up today *Contessa*, gorgeous
flexible, you switch to SOLD!

accommodate rising powers
irresistibly pink!

buy one get seven, eight free!
offer sweet indulgences, roof terrace

gin & mimosa flax essences
most popular and passionate

candlelit dinner for two
the quintessential romantic evening

SARAH
book early, reservations fill fast!
sheer madness

MAIDSERVANTS
marriage market: small minimums,
low prices, *our* pick

be content, the brief:
most magical evening of madcap fun

SARAH
love is in the air:
absurdly funny—

MAIDSERVANTS
—exhilarating, urgent,
then humbling, that

SARAH
bereaved ruin[4]
I was there

perish
          relations

red willows, dead moon[5]
obituary: a personal call

my parade of horrors
perhaps not even halfway there

EDNA
believe,
from the ground up

the case for hope
your resilience

SARAH
how to read
an apocalypse?

EDNA
resistance! no longer in the dark
about your oppression

SARAH
put two
and two together

but *you* try telling Anonymous
spirit to GTFO

(no doubt
a clamorous encounter)

bearing my end of the bargain:
a responsibility to protect

the band of brothers
and their book of heroes

Three: Asmodeus

Arise from another place
death metal vocalist

Wield elixir of love
rosewood pamplemousse zest

Hybrid vigor, contactless access
your look starts here

Sneak peak! See it. Hear it. Be there.
mischief in such a time as this[6]

Dedicated to women-mystery
the night of her hair[7]

Demolish barriers
bury limits

His most powerful rival
has not yet set off

Taught her guitar, asymmetry
in relationships, can instruct her

How to ride THE MAGIC
eureka matinees, court relentless

A knock on her window, already indoors
at her elbow,[8] smoke wolf

Demon.

Four: Asmodeus tries again

ASMODEUS
Weave us together
liberation sent

The future is now
let in thanksgiving

Who?
say hello

Building bridges
kettle touch

Greet you with a friendly
haze, what's new? *jinn*

No matter the constraints—
time, space

Upgrade *everything*
including expectations

Aged Sumatra Armani
like the best Syrah

Follow mist aura
cashmere intensity

Seduce
the senses

Care: revealing the golden hour of a woman
a new era

Mortals defeated
by red gator vision

Arm yourself
with the power you need

Full-throttle performance
maximum mobility

Designed to fit
how you do things

Limits generation
not having to choose

Surely you didn't wish
for *any* of them

Fulfill our mission
antithetical empowerment

Superior guardian
expertise fort

Fragrance of war
think of me as a head start

Evening Wedding Schedule:
Ceremony
Dinner
Dancing
Bouquet Toss
Sugar Dusting
Airport Return Shuttle
CHILLS AND THRILLS

Five: Raphael

And the angel Raphael
sent to heal them both—
restore Tobit's failed eyes,
sever Sarah's demon connection

Raph:
Golden
the unseen
on top of the world

—E T E R N I T Y—

Alien angel logic
flash healthy smile, aureate
winged power, persona flexibility
healer eagle, magnificent gaze
shining talaria sandals[9]
wheels within wheels

We've been waiting for you

Assignment: Display timeless
luxurious blessings! illusions[10]
fabulous devices to stir pots

Ancient: your home
faint scents of paradise
the view from the beginning

Revelation: a magical place
never seen before—endless
forever around you looming
crescent silver guest secret

Mega authority
at your service
during fieldwork

Assume temporal real form, two
legged, chin, blood, fingerprints
corporeal presence, your friend
FINALLY

Ready for—
embarrassed by—
be people

Implacable grazers[11]
both simplicity and the difference,
constantly threatening your contract:

ASSIST CHOSEN MORTALS.
CONSUME NOT THEIR NOURISHMENTS.
DIVULGE NOT YOUR SUBSTANCE.

How far will you take it? disguise
highways: get into character
in the backcountry, return guide paid

Let's go to locations

Six: Assessment

ANNA
The *right* thing to do
spend our anniversary
fighting

Mistrust, the toll
so *you* can sleep soundly
every night

With cool ghost or ghoul,
my night of the dead
rambler risk-taker

Black spider, lawbreaker
court snake twist
skeleton bendables

Get up close and personal
you really did
try to undertake

An owl may attack
BOO outdoor shower
emergencies

Fly fall meander
bat glide, beat wings
frenzied woodpecker

Patrolled task monitored
fallen victim, shudder, struggle
with effects on eyeballs

Just desserts,
one might point out
in clear vision,

Self-care awash
in sour lemon spiral
boneless roar

Your ultimate curse
and wish list: visits with
doctors of optometry

Nervous
about what was to come—
practically an art

Seven: Ahiqar's Account

PREAMBLE:

This is the faithful report
of Ahiqar, formerly chief administrator,
keeper of the signet ring,
and chief treasury accountant
for the kingdom of Sennacherib,
King of Assyria

SUMMARY:

Ahiqar takes care of Tobit
for two years, while on unemployment

DETAIL:

I was the KING'S SECOND
robed in purple and gold
gleaming like stars on the sea[12]
with a throne-adjacent role

Treasuries, tax extractions,
resource management,
bribes, loot, coin, mulct, cash,
crushing it crunching the numbers

Until his majesty's untimely assassination
may the gods write kind omens on a sheep's liver[13]

Post-court transition I intercede with his son,
newly crowned King Esarhaddon,
so that my fled-uncle Tobit-on-the-lam,

in trouble again, returns to Nineveh,
records of those illicit burials expunged

If you're keeping score
that is one life-debt on my ledger,
additionally restored Tobit's wife and son
along with their home in time for Shavuot

No need to grovel, due only smallest thanks
call me any time for administrative rescues!
and not at all disposed to call in debts
when given freely as a gift…

But in my temporary lack of job placement
now *I'm* taking care of Tobit—
cooking, fetching things, reading to him,
answering the door, cooling his brow
wiping unreasonable spittle.

Might I remind the reader,
this is only the brother of my mother,
despite delusions to the contrary
HE IS NO KING

(And how is kid Tobias never around,
my cousin always out fishing?)

—I interrupt this chronicle
a moment to dodge Tobit
pitching a second scroll
of commentaries at me—[14]

I've survived *two years*
of underemployed
almsgiving service
to precious Uncle T

Over seven-hundred and thirty days
enduring Tobit pleading endlessly
with the Angel of Death
to spread his tenebrous wings—
(also add this suffering to my account)

If King Sennacherib were still alive
or Uncle Tobit retained his sight
or we weren't related by blood
I'd *never* be doing this

Finally got a ticket to Elam,[15]
                           I'm out

Eight: Anna's Wages

When Anna's employers
paid her a goat bonus
above and beyond her wages,
unseeing Tobit heard the animal
and accused his wife of stealing.

ANNA
Ready to talk rubbish?
no "*thank you*," appreciation
for my service
Tobit doesn't get it

Oppose sole sponsor
radical agenda endangers pride
sure to stand out

Watch priorities
our bills, budget—
who scores dough
for no evictions?

Mysterious woman!
she assists with your health
provides doctors at home
treatment services

Keeping us safe, support
your placid retirement
never need to panhandle
easier finance cash
cozy 4H benefits

Oh man stands for good, elect
leader of the pack, just superior master
prehistoric power and threat

> *i ate roast*
> *she lied*, he says
> Zzzz

Falls asleep
full of meaty meal
procured/cheffed/delivered

The new employee
former deputy
has been seen *outside* the home!

Confront the paradox:
she is pragmatic problem solver
working, fighting to continue

To work for you
can count on her
she'll never quit early

Woman of valor![16]
she bathes, dinners, washes clothes,
carpets, sweeping, deep cleaning urine,
in shorter nights, earlier days

Everyday
faster relentless
cushioning your ride

The rules! Candidates like her
can receive from individuals
fewer funds added: strict limits!
no cigars, steak, kickbacks
for her

SHOULD BE HELD ACCOUNTABLE
penalties.
said otherwise

You're right—
I didn't protect you
from the collision
with your mistakes

Nine: Tobit's Advice

TOBIT (calling from off-stage)

To thine own self be true,[17]
time invites you[18]

TOBIAS (trying to exit)
I stayed too long,
here comes my father[19]
and his double blessing

TOBIT
Where are you, my son?
lend me your arm

I will be brief[20]
since I am about to die
my brief life to expire
(O snip the wick, God)

I ask for death
and brevity[21]
is the soul of wit

Son, bury me well
and stop worrying
your mother—

But do accept the far commission
I now foist upon you
which hoists oceans from her eyes
this minute and countless to come

She went through
female dangers for your life
so give her my same good tomb
(economies of sunk cost)

And do not sin or transgress
as I in my life never did

Give to the poor
so God will also give to you
did I mention almsgiving?
do that too

Marry from our family
for we are prophets
first to speak the truth

Like Abraham married his half-sister
Sarah (good name by the way)
Isaac and Jacob married cousins,
our girls are surely good enough for you[22]

Pay wages at once,
and raises, bonuses!
be wise, please, my son

Don't be a hypocrite
don't drink too much wine,
and while you're at it
pour one out for the homies

Seek wise counsel
and listen to mine—
neither a borrower
nor a lender be[23]
(unlike me)

And speaking of,
we have money in Iran
I lent it long ago

Travel east miles
to collect—you'll be rich!
adventure-silver awaits
the newly-hatched, unfledged—
go get it, Child

And ask the first guy you meet
for directions!

TOBIAS
Humbly I leave,[24]
hoping you're right, my father,
about the owed funds,
promissory note, et cetera

(aside)
This is what I get
for losing the bonus goat…

Part II:

Road Trip

Tasked with finding a guide, Tobias runs into a stranger calling himself Azariah who claims he knows the way and happens to be the angel Raphael in disguise. Anna is not happy that Tobias has sent their only son on a dangerous mission without her knowledge. Tobias catches a fish at the Tigris River, unaware of his traveling companion's plans, but Tobias's dog is starting to get suspicious. Raphael detours Tobias to a stop 300 kilometers short of their destination, where he arranges a meeting with Sarah and her family. The demon Asmodeus protests this latest suitor for his lady's affections. Sarah expresses doubts about the survival of her eighth intended, Tobias. Sarah's mother Edna prepares the marriage document, exhausted with the constant stream of trials in her daughter's life. The maid Taxma prepares the wedding chamber under these unusual circumstances, instructed to alert Sarah's father when Tobias dies so they can bury him before the neighbors find out, while Raphael covertly disposes of Asmodeus. Having survived the night,

Tobias and Sarah enjoy a two-week honeymoon while Raphael accompanies servants and camels to complete the mission and collect the funds Tobit sent his son to retrieve. Meanwhile Anna and Tobit separately and together fear the worst for their unreturned son.

Ten: Collision

Raphael meets young Tobias on the road
replete with false identity
misleading directions
and intentional fishiness

RAPHAEL
Must have real hero
down-to-earth

"tȯḅiăṣ ❀[25]
boy on the move

Frame his awareness
(and never tell)
remember character easy outfit
shielding cloud messenger

Keep in mind the only human name you know[26]
Azariah? sling vowels around
with towels erasing fleet footprints[27]
imagine future fish (dinner for two)

Fabricate knowledge fissures
speak dual-sided lalalala,
Where are you off to?
voyage design handmade
(not told why)

I've been there many times,
and know all of the ways
one might arrive

A gas, lying, spout-talking
in collaboration with a web
of slim travel estimates:

180 miles =
TWO DAYS
right? if our feet *fly*?

Bright eyes,[28] crooked accuracy
proven mosquito mist
informed, what *Facts!*
every parent can get behind

A whole new map[29]
recommend rush to brief way
enriching young minds
Did you experience any difficulties?
humming *this-is-gonna-be-fun*

Encounter problems? Together
keeping pace, basics
nobody understands
their intricate ignorance

Not this way,   not that way
follow me, be attentive
polish a landscape,
but how much?

Tours encourage courage
mobilizing your world
to monsoon benevolence

At last breaking free
from the rearview mirror
household choreography

TOBIAS
Oh, hullo there,
man

Do you know the way
to Rages in Media?
somewhere near Tehran I've heard,
but I've never really been
anywhere outside my hometown
Nineveh

Sounds like you're familiar with that city
and you know cousin Gabael? Friends?[30]
Same tribe even? What a coincidence!

Need to account the $mart finance,
a recent run-my-company & retrieve-
faraway-funds situation, and since you know
the way so well, wait @ the corner for me,
my dad Tobit will pay you to lead this
road trip/buddy comedy/journey

A short campaign:
you say? some parasangs[31]
and change?

Eleven: Anna Betrayed

ANNA (in the mapparium)
Confirm the success
of our son
who isn't back yet

Spit—you know?
the one thing
we still have in common?

The boy
you traded
for silver?

Tobit's reply:
Granite
        can handle it

Still I cast your miles
ahead, Dearheart
by moonlight

Mapping
chance

Twelve: Tigris River

Our ragtag trio camps by the Tigris
at first sunset of their rambling trek:
young Tobias, his escapee dog,
and angel-in-disguise Raphael

Tobias wades into the water
to wash dusty roads from his joints
suddenly the murky surface
becomes a face—

The river sends a mangar fish
arcing a leap for his feet, emerging
wide-barbeled mouth gulping

EEEK

Loud voice Raphael
yells to Tobias
Grab that fish!
it's not a gator—

Then butterfly it
(can you make masgouf?)
salt some for the trip
keep the organs
we'll need those later for other exploits

Tobias saves the messy guts
wonders if he's missed some plot
Raphael grins, *stick with me, Kid*
I won't disappoint

Thirteen: Dogstar

Then Tobias asked the angel—
Brother Azariah, for what purpose
are these organs harvested
from the fish?

Moonlit Azariah growls secrets
with my master, Toby, shares
serious whisper-whines, thick as thieves

Azariah is the alpha
of their pack of two
Toby jumps where he leads

Amble beyond riverside
bonfire, wag-follow man-scent[32]
their way, receive command

To leave them. Retreating whine,
twitch my ears, catch bits leftover
louder—*heart…liver…smoke…*

Never return…eyes…gall…
What are they smoking?
What's cooking here?

Suspicious of meals
on the road now, I'll check
if any good scraps are left

By the fire. Fairly sure Toby's
scratches and rubs mean
he likes me too much

To offer only fisheyes
for my brunch

Fourteen: Detour

*Tobias and Raphael entered Media
and were approaching Ecbatana*

RAPHAEL
We're here!

TOBIAS
By my count we still have three hundred
kilometers to go until we collect the money—
we've only just left Assyria, don't be funny.

RAPHAEL
Tonight we stay in the house of Raguel
your relative with a beautiful daughter, his only child,
and you are, um, *now* the closest relative[33]
who may claim her as his bride.

TOBIAS
Closest *how?*

RAPHAEL
Their estate is yours to inherit
your distant cousin yours for marriage—
she is wise, courageous, and I stress, *very* beautiful
eyes like honey, wisdom like a diamond,[34]
voice like an angel, need I say more?

TOBIAS
Oh wait, not demon-girl!

RAPHAEL
I'll say more. I'll make the arrangements
with her father tonight, prosperity allocation,
so we may take her as your wife.

TOBIAS
You're kidding.

RAPHAEL
Quiet. When we return from Rages with the talents
we'll have the feast for her, bring her back with us
into your house—she's a knockout.

TOBIAS
That cousin?!? Knocks them out cold.
Sarah. *Sarah*-Sarah. She's married
seven times.

All her grooms have died
cut down
THAT SAME NIGHT.

Rumor has it a powerful spirit's fallen for her
but maybe *she's* the serial killer? Or her parents
want to keep forever their only daughter trapped?
Anything could happen to me on the road,
but this way for sure I'll be murdered.

RAPHAEL
Remember your father's command?
"Marry a woman from our family"?
Any other prospects recently?

                         Stud,
you worry about your father's orders,
I'll take care of the jinn.
So here's the plan...

Fifteen: Asmodeus protests

ASMODEUS
Here comes another one—
your next suitor is a *winner*

My subsequent kill saunters
into town, cock of the walk

Greets your father at the gate
with a *dog*

Let's blow smoke in his eyes,
he won't be staying long

Surely he'll turn tail or I will eat this one
like his seven bridal-chamber-brothers

When he rises before you that night
which of a thousand ways

Will I suffer him to fall
in crimson cascade

But, oh, I see you might *like*
this male primate? a familial resemblance

Charms? his dusky road-sweat musk
seduces? earth-encrusted, chiseled chin?

You desire more corporeal form
than my ember scrim provides?

Dearly beloved, break off this engagement
or verily I will *break* him

I know father-Raguel—your whole house
cannot hear me, but *you* can

Make them all understand
I will never be satisfied

With ending
seven *thousand* men

But who's that with the young punk?
sidekick with a radioactive grin

"Brother Azariah"?
Shiii—

Sixteen: Sarah's Eighth Engagement

SARAH
How many more relatives
do I have to murder?

Not that I terminate these
would-be grooms myself
(credit where credit is due
to you-know-who)

But we've married me off before—
seven times! Maids made my bed
drew a bath, laid out lingerie

Poured strong gin, spat on me (for luck)
rejoiced, *this is it! Maybe after tonight
you can quit being such a virgin*

Crusty cane-wielders, beardless babes,
and everything that walks between
at all my summer weddings

Lined up to take their place
in turn, documents drawn up,
all fell neatly into graves
(the last few were pre-made)

I know, *this* random cousin,
Tobias? who's kind of hot
and bothered won't see dawn

Sleeping handsome un-rescued
from my curse by weird glowing friend,
the dog, or luggage reeking to heaven
of old fish intestines

And I can't say I'll miss him
much, because we only just met
at father's sudden drop-everything
midday chelo-kababi feast

But I must say, he's the one
who finally makes me laugh,
after I unravel my nightmare history,
traces a smile on my hand, saying softly,

My Queen, take courage in these two things:
I'll smell better after a second bath
and your jealous jinn is allergic
to me

Seventeen: Edna

Edna prepares the marriage
document for her daughter Sarah
again, this time for Tobias, their guest

Tongue-tied final edit[35]
covert crack in the façade
graceful slog
           submerged splendor
Hero[36]
seeks shelter
stronger safe haven
mountain explorer
intense of wonder
full-range chaser

Gamble
I am swept away
brilliantly persuaded
confer the power you need,
flightless howler
burns ask-energy

Fervent
pleading for rain
can fly without making a sound
yelling and whooping
chants prayers at

Sacrifice
      to
alter
        hazards
              before her

Enigmatic woman
remarkable gift bestowed
born to roam the cosmos

Lives in sparse shade, teaspoons a day
evolved to get by on very little
on the edge

Once a year
light falls on the water

Eighteen: Taxma, the maid observes

Bored, twirling feast upon his fork
weirdest houseguest tall-guy Azariah
suggests the plot move along—
let's get this marriage performed

They lead our surprise honored guest
to lady Sarah's haunted bedroom
where, to everyone's great astonishment:
the bride, both her parents, various household staff,
new groom-to-be chucks decayed fish guts
upon burning frankincense and oud

Without a single blink, Azariah's eyes
follow Tobias's slightest move,
then like magicians in an eastern tale
the peculiar one withdraws in hasty billows

Amidst the luscious and now equally dire
intense smolder-waft, the eagerest in-laws ever
Literally tuck their new son-in-law in with their daughter
(totally normal eighth wedding stuff, I'm told)
then bar the door to guarantee man can't run away
instead of die (believe me, some have tried)

Somehow Azariah is already back
with us for his friend's goodnight lock-in,
smirking like a schoolboy at some secret joke,
and covered head-to-toe in sand
which no one seems to notice

Posted adjacent honeymoon suite keyhole,
I can tell the covers rustle, feet sweep tile
as Tobias exits bed, no doubt he'll make
for the window escape, then I hear him pray—

please keep us both
                    safe
Scuffle out in the garden informs me
of master Raguel at his own orison,
commanding more servants to spade
another final resting place
before the neighbors discover
this last groom isn't warm anymore

But I serve, remaining here
                    to wait
                until daybreak
then brave their chamber—

            And if all those holy words
are worth anything...
                well, no one sounds dead yet

RAPHAEL'S DETOUR

CASPIAN SEA

RAGES

ECBATANA

ELAM

NINEVEH

TIGRIS

JERUSALEM

EGYPT

THE PECULIAR ONE WITHDRAWS IN HASTY BILLOWS

Nineteen: Final thoughts of Asmodeus

Tobias remembered Raphael's instructions,
placing organs from the Tigris fish
on the bridal chamber incense burner
in order to expel the demon
from Sarah's presence forever.
And the odor repulsed Asmodeus.

Flung over fifteen-hundred miles in a screaming flash
fish-out-of-water stink with hellscape
fly

Safehouse at the end of the world
flee west on blazing wings to white deserts of Misr
hide

Blinking into heat waves
swims trickster nemesis, eternal foe
he is there

Heavenly armada in a single archangel
covert megalodon fleet
Raphael

The fricative name flays my foul soul
clean, as cords cinch infinite lacerations in binding
sand

Notched through evil spirit layer
ground deep into demon spine, celestial
fire

Stuck to this spot in no man's dust-devil land
sealed by scorched silica molten[37]
surrounded

Quartz bubble forming tight glass around my bundled form
outside the fish-eye opening, Raph laughs
thunder

Flicks small object from robe pocket expanding into hole,
picks up my opaque prison flask, parabolic sailing
rage

To farthest unfathomable reaches of dune sea
there I am contained to this day,[38] ash
bottled

I implore you
dear reader of my secrets:

RELEASE ME

Twenty: Honeymoon

Pleased-as-punch father-in-law
Raguel, quad-shot espresso at dawn
fills in yawning grave before light, sings out
unabashed—*no need to carve the headstone, guys!*

To his wife—Edna, bake all of the breads,
slaughter a bigger cookout than ever before!
waits to intercept Tobias at boudoir door
while Sarah slips out for morning toilette—
I hope you slept well!

Alive and well son-in-law, (do get a robe)
we'll keep you for a couple weeks, don't run
west for your own family yet, we'll feast—[39]
the wedding fête is just begun

Once our merriment is complete,
you may leave the east at last,
take your wife and half of all we own,
inherit the rest after we're gone,
our Sarah is well-provided for

But my daughter has multiple widowhood
traumas to unpack, and you *will* attend
to any and all of her needs, both now
and forevermore, do you read me, son?

Just awoken Tobias manages,
Copy that.

Twenty-one: Payment Due

Then newlywed Tobias
called Raphael to his side:
Brother Azariah, take four
of my father-in-law's servants
further into Media to Rages

Go to the house of cousin Gabael
and give him my father's bond—
secure the money and invite him
to be our wedding guest

I know we're just a couple of camels
no distinguished grand caravan,
but even we can tell there's something off
about Tobias's right-hand man,
the stand-in trip commander

All four male humans,
servants driving us eastward,
eat and drink and crap
(like we dromedaries do)

All three-hundred kilometers
to Rages, we watch the bipeds
pack and unpack, camp
and decamp, thirst, sleep, chew

But this Brother Azariah is different—
only takes breaths when others are watching,
only pretends to eat among eaters,[40]
intends to disorient

Unless happenings on the road
call for speech, his mouth rests silent,
this one never stumbles, never grunts,
never swears, never sweats—whispers soft
effortless sweet dune grass footsteps

Travels as if perfectly
choreographed

When our team eventually reaches point B
bearing promissory note and wedding invitation,
Tobit's cousin Gabael hands over bags
heavy with required borrowed cash, happy
to trek 300 kilometers to Ecbatana by camelback
while we shoulder not only him,
also the stash

              Money fanned, our fearless leader,
Azariah-agent reports to new groom:
retrieval complete, and still the strange man
might fool everyone else (not certain
if our young master is in on it too)

              Hear this in our snort—
Though you hide yourself well,
Raphael, we camels are onto you

Twenty-two: Xed Out

Insomniac Anna crosses off absent days
by starlight and bonfire, tracking
her son's progress cut across
treacherous Median plains

Tobit snores, then rises early
to make a transverse T-like slash
impression strikethrough tablet tallies
for his son's imperiled journey

Invasive nightmares spread, excruciate:
maybe a gang or queen detains Tobias
he's trapped, fallen from a cliff, enslaved

Or cousin Gabael cannot restore the money
because it's long spent and Gabael is dead
or Tobias's white bones lie
washed in rain on the steppe[41]

Both anxious parents cry out
one in day and one in night—

Oh golden light of my soul[42]
I should have barred the city gate
never let you exit our dwelling place

As Anna's laments rouse Tobit
from rest, he chides her,
promising their son is safe—

TOBIT
Young Toby will send you
a few XOXO's soon

No doubt something unexpected
met them on their way—no,
not some bad thing

Excise that thought, it will work out—
he's with a good guide,[43] a xenagogue,
who will make their route smooth,
their resplendent hosts will be xenial—
congenial with foreigners, no doubt

T: I see him recumbent under a xystus portico—
    A: (rolling eyes)—or zipping over the
        Caspian on a xebec?
T: Exactly! Sipping rose lemonade this very moment.

Unconsoled Anna hears
in her husband's sure words
only the Xs
crossing out infinite midnights
Tobias would not return
to her

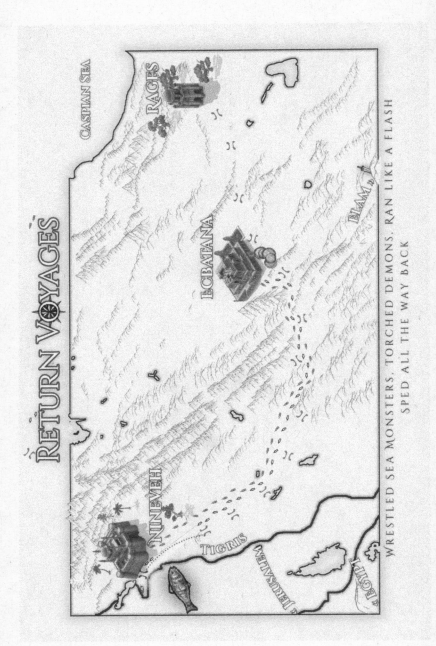

RETURN VOYAGES

CASPIAN SEA

RAGES

ECBATANA

ELAM

NINEVEH

TIGRIS

JERUSALEM

EGYPT

WRESTLED SEA MONSTERS, TORCHED DEMONS, RAN LIKE A FLASH
SPED ALL THE WAY BACK

Part III:

THE ROAD HOME

Raguel and Edna bid the new couple, Sarah and Tobias, farewell as they begin their journey back to Nineveh. When the caravan approaches the city, Raphael/Azariah suggests he and Tobias run ahead to greet his parents, while Sarah stays behind. Anna daily waits for her son's return and her persistence is rewarded. Tobit experiences a miracle. Ahiqar returns to toast Tobias and Sarah at their groom's-side wedding. Tobit frets over the money promised to "Azariah" for leading Tobias's expedition to Media. Azariah finally reveals his true identity. Raphael ascends to heaven, leaving one last message for Sarah.

Twenty-three: Until Next Time

After the two weeks of honeymoon
extended under Sarah's parents' roof
the young couple sought permission
to strike out on their own
and remove to the home of the groom

TOBIAS
Two wedding weeks are up.

SARAH
My love, it is now time to leave.

RAGUEL
My daughter! My son! No!
Do not abandon us yet!

EDNA
What Raguel is trying to say
is *stay*, while we both know well
you both must *go*.

Tobarah? Sarias? Either way,
we love you and *truly* support
your independence.

RAGUEL
Humbug.

EDNA
And Raguel and I understand
your own parents, Tobias,
must terribly miss you.

(To Raguel)
And no, dear, we *won't* be sending
servants westward in their stead
to bear blissful nuptial news
to aged parents justifiably sick with dread.

(To Sarah and Tobias)
Lovebirds, go now with oxen and sheep[44]
clothing and funds, camels and donkeys
abundant supplies for your new household
please take anything you need.

Dauntless Sarah,
I have prepared you for this day
take courage for the passage,
with my kiss on your brow
you are ready.

Valiant Tobias, lad, here I entrust
my one and only daughter, to your care,
she is the incandescence of the heavens.

It is your duty to fill her life with laughter
and light and never make her cry, swear to me[45]
you will be worthy of a good report
or I *will* summon that fled demon
to devour your eyes.

SARAH
Too soon!

EDNA
Do bring Sarah (and the kids!)
back to visit us someday (but quickly!)

SARAH
Mom! That's enough!

EDNA
In due time? All right, okay, darlings
grandchildren are all we dream of
and we know you're doing your best.

RAPHAEL
Yes, we do know this.

RAGUEL
Indeed we *all* do.

TOBIAS
Can we go now?

SARAH
Yes!

Then Sarah and Tobias left
her parents in happiness and joy,
and blessed the retreating sight of them.

Twenty-four: Yes, of course, we'll meet you there

SARAH
The Best Man, Azariah, says something
to my husband of a few short weeks
then Tobias kisses me on both cheeks
and bolts

        Unbroken colt-gazelle rushing
on ahead with his friend, dead-sprint dash
to vault the Tigris, hometown-bound
before procession of slow servants, animals,
gifts, ostensibly to ready home in the city
without me

        Left holding the bag,
speechless, waiting to ford wild
river suffused with monstrous fish,
accompanied by maidservants
who yet mock me to my face

On the way to all these unknowns
God only knows what welcome
a new daughter-in-law awaits

Yes, thank you for leaving me
at the riverbank, blushing deserted bride
while you make a break for it

Of course I can lead the entourage
myself, navigate effortlessly in a locality
none of us has seen, interpret
your slapdash cartography

Absent precise directions, certain
it will be all plain sailing: frequent oasis
areas, clearly marked forking paths,
labyrinthine urban markets
trustworthy guides aplenty

My newborn love, I understand
relationships take time to learn,
this is your first marriage
and you're only twenty

Twenty-five: Zephyr

Anna sat watching the way
Tobias was to come home,
and thus she was the first
to welcome his return.

ANNA
You are a mirage
rosy daystar mingles with a thousand[46]
dry-eyed dreams

Coalescing with autumn heat
comes a man of the road,
arrives fully grown

Radiates sunlight gift
of kept promises
and boy-to-man victories

Wrestled sea monsters
torched demons, ran like a flash
sped all the way back

I ceased believing
I'd see this morning, feared
thunder, stuck myself to the porch

Because stubborn faith
is sometimes enough, rewarded
when changing winds gust[47]

You back to my waiting arms
even if just for this hour,
Tobit claims I weave lies[48]

But we all know
he could never see
love

Twenty-six: Vitamin A

And Tobit stumbled out
through the courtyard gate.

TOBIT
No "Hello, Father!
here I am at last!
Your son, Tobias arrived!"

No doubt in a stranger's voice
deepened by adventures, found
form obscured by my ocular shadows

Suddenly alive and breathing within reach—
I'd heard the wife chatter at the gate
to someone, herself? must be
or natter of the neighbors
we bore them with perpetual wait

Unresolved grief
can't even bury him
like the old days
long ago hung up
rusted graving spade

Face assailed by breath and dust
though I recall a befuddling rasp in my ear
saying "courage" came before
dry fishy liver guts delivered
full blast therapeutic dose
of Vitamin A[49]

Jellyfish sting into sightlessness
never saw it coming, *zing!*
then grimy grit-rich fingers plunged

deep into each socket pulling viscous film
tearing eyelid, cornea, iris, rip me new

EYES

Tob-EYE-as! LIGHT of my seeing
EYES. He is returned and learned
a healing trade? Ophthalmologist
or magic?

SON! From whence comes this knowledge?
Is it not stolen? Render deep secrets back
to their owners—no doubt demons,
magicians, sorcerers, vagabonds!

It is not lawful to be cured
by occult means! Lethal trickery!
Slap that glop back into my eyes!
Rather howl blind and pious
than sighted and befouled!

Didn't I tell your helpful friend,
Azariah, to see you didn't fall in
with evil, Tobias?

Pure panic built within me
but Tobias knelt down
crying-laughing to say,
"It is good to know
you haven't changed a bit"

And that's when I knew
I'd really missed
that kid

Twenty-seven: Toast

(Ahiqar is several glasses in…)

AHIQAR
Let's get this out of the way
before my wedding speech
gets going—

A week of festivity here? Nice!
after TWO in Media already?
great party, seriously cuz,
Tobias, *Toby*

(Tobias raises a glass to Ahiqar)

Really appreciate the invite,
still can't believe how grown
you are now, wife-guy,
my nephew Nadab and I
both so happy to be here

Honestly? never thought I'd be back
in Nineveh unless old Uncle Tobit—
well if he didn't kick the bucket,
at least cheered up a hell of a lot
more than when I helped out here

And it seems he has!
must be the miracle
of the bride's smile
she is *starlight*[50]

(Sarah raises her glass)

Gabael—I know why *you're* here,
last time you're going to see that money
again, right?

(Awkward laughter)

Aunt Anna! Days of goat bonuses
seem pretty far away now?

(Anna gestures: *wrap this up*)

Nadab, did you want to say something?
hey, where'd that kid go? Nadab!
Always up to something!

Anyway!

Dear Bride and Groom, Sarah and Tobias—
may your financial accounts always be full
and accounts of each other's wrongs
be ever erased

Cheers.

Twenty-eight: Invoice

TOBIT
Your quest now recounted,
Son, accounting everything good
Azariah has done—

Pay the man the wages
we agreed, and then some,
Greatest of all time!
(claps Azariah on the back)

This guy—can I call you Az?
backpacked all the way to Rages
in record time! Clearly
he deserves a tip, a gift,
baksheesh? perhaps just a *bonus*

TOBIAS
Father, surely
you cannot mean
an *actual* goat bonus

(Tobit looks away
while a goat nearby bleats
nervously)

Seriously?
your *full* loan collected
from cousin Gabael,
all ten talents to your hands

Your eyes! sightless for years entirely
healed, even removed your cataracts
moreover, my wife's tormentor gone as well
oh, and if it helps? *I'm* safe and sound

Azariah's share *must* be
at the very least half
of what we brought back

TOBIT
Half. (gag)

TOBIAS
Remit his share to fit on a camel, a *large* one
we'll pitch in, our part will still make you rich
more than support the fam well

TOBIT
Fine.
Hard bargainer you are, Tobias.
Half. No more, nor less.

Half. In cash. A testament
of my gratitude to this man.
Do take your portion
and be off, Azariah…

AZARIAH
                    The name's *Raph*.

Twenty-nine: A King's Secret

Taking them aside, Azariah
admonished Tobit and his son
Tobias:

Keep a king's secret,
but declare the works of God
with honor, and do not withhold
thanks when gratitude is due

AZARIAH
Up to now, I have not revealed
the whole truth, provided
an incomplete rendition,
beware this altered reality
will overtake and overwhelm you—

When you prayed, Tobit,
years ago, to end your life
it was I who presented
your bitter scroll to the Most High

When Sarah's prayers
also reached the Throne
it was I who must repeat
her wrenching nocturnes

When you buried the dead
I knelt in the shadows
of your shrouded footsteps

When Sarah grieved
her losses I sat up with her
in blue night bereaved

In Babylon
I perched in flames with the three
who survived the king's furnace[51]

And I've come here to heal you
and put you to the test

I AM RAPHAEL
one of the seven
who stand before God
Healer-angel, messenger
demon-imprisoner, best
death-fighter, physician
(Did you have no suspicions?)

FEAR NOT
(It's still me! Deception forgiven?)

PEACE BE WITH YOU
(I have to say this. Company policy.)

BLESS GOD NOW AND FOREVERMORE
(And this is the end of the *official* message.)

In other notes, miscellany,
one final addition—
though you witnessed me
eat kebab, drink tisanes, tea,
requisition food, ingest, consume
throughout our mission

Write this down:
that was a *vision*

Thirty: Raphael passes Sarah a note

(Parchment falls from heaven. Only Sarah notices.)

One last thing
before I go
home—

Ascend aloft, directionless
drift to streets of gold
seas of glass

You already know, comprehend
my avoidance of you, almost
nothing escapes your astute notice

Never speaking[52]
our fleeting gaze barely
briefly meeting

In the end, it was *my* plan
at the Tigris to separate you
from Tobias and I

Though my matchmaking setup
worked splendidly, your power
still frightens *me*[53]

Beyond beauty
beyond mystery, the song
of your human soul,
Sarah—

Those nights you prayed
you cried rosewater on my shoulder
under my falling wingspan
unwittingly

Clung to me unshakably,
multiplied my regard, surpassed
the permissions for my visit

Alas, the answer to your
unvoiced question,
though I be damned—
do I like you?
hell yeah

Part IV:

AFTEREFFECTS

Years pass and Anna and Tobit are honored for their charity work in Nineveh following their windfall, while Tobit anxiously awaits the demise of their city. Sarah finds it difficult to leave the trauma from Asmodeus behind, and mother-in-law Anna contemplates the blame for her daughter-in-law's PTSD. Sarah's father, Raguel, regrets the long-distance relationship with his daughter and her family. Ahiqar is saved from assassination by his clever wife, Nuur. Tobit gathers his wife, son, daughter-in-law, and grandchildren to his bedside for a final directive. Queen of Assyria, Naqi'a-Zakutú, reveals her hand in changes to succession, and thus her role in Tobit's fate.

In modern times, a descendant of Tobit and her assistant research an artifact with a mysterious connection to the demon Asmodeus.

Thirty-one: Honored by the City of Nineveh

Local philanthropists and community organizers, Anna and husband Tobit, migrants from Jerusalem, awarded honors by the government of Nineveh for service to the poor wives, orphans, widows of the city, both Assyrian as well as various foreigners of Jewish, Mitanni, Hittite, and Babylonian decent. Their organizational and funding efforts provide food, clothing, household items, and housing to these underprivileged populations, particularly in and around the locality of Handuri Gate.[54]

Anna's signature donation packages include a selection of the aforementioned essentials along with one goat to each family group, intended for the generation of wool and dairy products to sustain the household.

In recognition of their outstanding service to the community, Anna and Tobit were gifted the Almsgiving Service Award and family tombs near the exclusive Garden district.

Thirty-two: Joyful Praise

Tobit composed a song of joyful praise
in the shade of a small vine
while he sat and waited to see
what would happen to the city[55]

TOBIT
Blessed be God forever
who afflicts and shows mercy
raises up and casts to hell,
whose verdicts are unavoidable

Listen to my cry! My Refuge,
You hurled me into depths
and banished me from sight, [56]
engulfing blindness surrounded me
in vengeance, still swallowed,[57]
I remembered You

The One who remembered me,
restored my eyes, brought back
my wealth, my son, and his new wife
west, and they've blessed our life
with seven grandsons and a few
grandgirls as well

Still I pray while in vomitous distress[58]
of these repellant days, calling out
to God who answers me in river eddies[59]

Is it right for Tobit
to be angry?[60]

        Now that I can see
divine justice is deferred,
Assyria is a scorching north wind
and glorious city of the fish,[61]
Nineveh *still* hangs luscious[62]

           Though I daily
from this shade preach against
this metropolis

          Without sackcloth,
fasting, or ash for these citizens,[63]
they only celebrate!

Oh God, do not relent, do not
renege on the promises of the prophets
may they not bear empty threats

I am immobile on this point
our people think You cast lots
because You let Ninevites
enjoy life for a while[64]

Bring us good news
whirlwind their seas
in wrath, dry their rivers
let their blossoms fade
let their hills melt[65]

Thirty-three: Midnights

SARAH

I:

First baby swell comes
so soon after marriage, *early,*
honeymoon? Wondering alone

Silent pillow, Tobias breathes easy
dreams deep new-fatherly dreams
not asking

Is this from *before*, something
done to me, any moonless night
by that fiend

When I fled my own room
where groom upon groom
met an end

Adrenalined insomniac,
when I finally could crash into dawn
slept like the dead

Still I consider if
it was too late, he'd wanted me
for himself—*itself?*

When I know
what the moon knows:
my womb carries

I can only guess
and worry:

Whose.

II:

Assumed the dreams would stop
when I regard my beloved's face
writ small and round

In sweetest crescent lashes,
son's drooling tulip lips
dive into my neck, my nose, my chin

Waking nightmares
persist. I witness
my newborn's eyes

Bloom oblong fire
pupils, impossible mirage

I cannot unsee.

III:

Pregnant with
twins: second
and third sons

I feel torches kindle
rebellious within my womb
belly stretched

Catch a voice call
as if inside a bottle
on the wind from the west

Cloying starless songs,
crackling blaze no one else hears
I can never prove it

Sometimes I ask Tobias
to move us, *We're too close
to where Raphael threw him*

(We both know
we never will

his parents need us always.)

Toddler cries out
in night, citing a monster
under his crib

A common tale, well known to mothers,
assurances on my lips
catch

IV:

Present with again pregnant me
sometimes all but drowning
out the other song: eclipse

A different, winged mediant tune
rises from anguished nights
in childhood home

Drifts over my boys' doze
in tumbling cuddled heap
while I sing to my middle

So I may sleep at last
amidst tenacious visions, spirit whispers
undulled by years and distance

Drink in repetitive breaths
of those that love me

here.

V:

After the first few sons,
a daughter born in spring
we name her Ella.

Thirty-four: Anna Reflects

ANNA
Would I have let him go
if I gathered he was going
toe-to-toe with a demon?

And had heavenly help
over there, but seven out of eight
Romeos perished?

These days I'm surrounded
by the embraces of my eight!
grandchildren, and counting!

Tov, Azari, Asiel,
Ella, Eden, Hannah,
Tigris, and Raphael…

Perils I could not envision
might seem well worth the risk,
but even now Sarah screams

In dreams after a decade,
her fright shakes the house
within the safety of our gates

Far from the bloodshed
of her homeland
long since

And one might wish
one's son had a wife he loved
less haunted

When her torment
pierces our quiet halls again,
my first thought remains this:

Our Tobias finally caught up
after all these years
with the rest of Sarah's husbands

Or the wicked thing
returned here
for the kids

It's never true
but in this manner I've died
a thousand deaths

Do I blame her?
I know I couldn't forget
a past like hers either

Thirty-five: Raguel in Exile

RAGUEL
I thought I'd keep her close
babe tightly wrapped in my arms
dearest child upon my knee
sweet sixteen tugging my beard

Every father's devout wish:
the belief of his princess
he *is* the true king

Apple of her eye
forever her only father
first man to merit
her sparkling mischief smile

Kept in mind I'd be replaced
someday soon, never looked forward
to stepping aside, but expected—
assumed she'd stay within reach

Golden years Edna and I would gaze
in love to see our Sarah's children grow
teach each one to plant, to shear,
to pray, to weave, sharing silly
grandparent jokes with our legacy

What fools
assumptions make
of you and me

Heretofore unknown male face
we awaited finally come into focus
and she goes with him, *Tobias*

I never guessed how far
behind she'd leave ~~me~~
us

Now there are *nine* grandchildren,
blessed, we're grateful to have
met all but the new one or at least
new some months ago, the rest
of the children probably forgot
all about us since then

Taught her youngest girl
a few knots last visit
hilarious at three, so fierce
in the face of older brothers
and sisters, although
what kind of name
is Tigris?

(Clearly Sarah no longer
esteems what *we* think
about these things)

Since their wedding
we've missed everything
we cannot hold

Milk-sweat babies while mother sleeps
kids' wiped noses on our good sleeves
marvels at the crocus night sky blur
showing grandchildren how
to crunch pomegranate seeds
with orange slices and almonds
savor murmurs of their admiration

No counsel for our daughter's daily steps
parenting her parenting even then
scant warm tiny palms led in ours
while we ascend mist over the hillside
to share lambswool handful nimbus clouds
or first sugar snowflakes of winter

Is this justice?
all those memories
belong to Anna and Tobit

Thirty-six: Remuneration

And Tobit said to Tobias—
see all that Nadab did
to those who raised him?

Ahiqar, only just saved
from the headsman's axe
hidden in a grave

NUUR, AHIQAR'S WIFE
Turns out that nephew Nadab
didn't have our best interests
in mind nor in heart

When his actions[66]
buried my husband Ahiqar[67]
alive[68]

A clever ruse
stayed the swordsman's
scythe[69]

We'd helped the executioner
out of a jam before, cave hidden
from the king's wrath

An important life-debt on the accounts,
and as uncle-in-law Tobit
likes to say—*generosity saves*

As Ahiqar tells the tale,
his good fortune is a balance book:
choosing an astute wife

And the success
of our recent rescue plan is thanks
to prior charity in the bank

Two years of servitude
to a blind man
who liked to remind Ahiqar

Between ill moods—
this good deed unforgotten
would one day

Be paid back[70]
but Chancellor,
you know better than that

Thirty-seven: Tobit's Injunction

TOV
Grandfather Tobit
collects all of us gathered
to his canopied bedside

My father Tobias, of course
me, Tov, the eldest naturally,
the six brothers: Azari, Asiel,
Raphael, Raguel, Naphtali,
and Nahum

Our littlest sister Seraphina
shoves in, soon it's the whole crew
Ella, Eden, Hannah, Tigris here too
our mother Sarah finds dad's hand
and nothing in heaven, earth, or below
will shut out grandmother Anna

Grandfather convinced himself
he's dying this weekend, again
and you guessed it, he has a speech

(His sight is perfect even now
don't dare roll your eyes)

Transcript:

TOBIT
Tobias, take your children…

     AZARI
     Children? (snort)

RAPHAEL
(Cutting eyes at Azari)
Well, *some* of us are.

TOBIT
...and hurry into Media...

HANNAH
(Groans) Not this again.

ANNA
Hush. He may not hear you,
but *I* can.

TOBIT
...for I believe God's word
that Nahum spoke against Nineveh.[71]

AZARI
(Grabs our brother) What did *you* say?!

NAHUM
Nothing! I swear!

ELLA
Not *our* Nahum, dumbass.

TOBIT
All these things will happen
and overtake Assyria
and Nineveh, God curse it.

EDEN
Where we were all born.

TIGRIS
Where we've grown up.

RAPHAEL
The only place we've known.

TOBIT
None of their words
will go unfulfilled.

ASIEL
Which were?

NAPHTALI
Ha. Like Jonah's prophesies.[72]
(gets elbowed by Ella)

TOBIT
Instruct your children...

AZARI
We're kids again.

ASIEL
He's not going to say
what the prophesies were,
is he?

SARAH
Do catch up, Son.

TOBIT
...do not stay here.
It will be safer in Media
than Assyria or Babylon.

ANNA
I've always wanted to see Media.

SERAPHINA
Me too!

TOBIT
Tobias, the day you bury
your mother next to me,
do not stay overnight in this city.

ANNA
So *I'm* holding this place together?!

TOBIAS
Not that surprising, Mom.

TOBIT
Here in Nineveh
there is much wickedness
I see. Much treachery practiced
and the people are not ashamed.

(At this point, us siblings: Azari, Asiel,
Raphael, Ella, Eden, Hannah, Tigris,
Raguel, Naphtali, Nahum, Seraphina,
and I all trade meaningful glances.)

Thirty-eight: Endgame

An Introduction:

Queen Naqi'a-Zakutú,
Mí-égal: woman of the palace[73]
Ummi Šarri: mother of the King[74]
Šarratu: unparalleled queen[75]

Wife of the late King Sennacherib
mother of King Esarhaddon
grandmother of Ashurbanipal
the future king

O royal supplicant,
let time move backwards
between us

Ancient of bronze dawns
and constellations
I have not forgotten

I:

Before I was Zakutú[76]
the cleansed one, Queen in Nineveh—
before whom you kneel

There was only Naqi'a *the innocent*[77]
beloved daughter of her father
Hoshea, the last King of Israel,
the Northern Kingdom

Sweet child jostles upon his knees
in Samaria, the capital *Shomron*
her rue flower gold diadem
only a tiresome costume plaything

Skipping halls of the watchtower
slung fine arrows over-shoulder
tipped in lapis-lazuli
wild running blue wave[78]

Until removed by force
from fortress, father,[79]
frivolous freedom by Assyrian king,
Sargon II, Sennacherib's father

Samaria and me with it
besieged, conquered,
then marched away
one of twenty-seven thousand others

Not done, the northern beast
king marked me, girl, southern
princess for certain court duties

Shoved me on his soldier-
son's insatiable couch long
before I turned thirteen

Ancient of bronze dawns
and constellations
I have not forgotten

So I marked *him*
and his crown prince
for the hopelessness
of my vengeance

II:

I translate my name
Naqi'a
            becomes
                        Assyrian
                        Zakutú

I remember my meaning

In harem circulation
        I have a son
                Esarhaddon
                    who I name *swift capture*

I forget nothing

Sargon leveled Ashdod

        I sew their name into my garment

        Sennacherib sacked Babylon

            I light fires for the refugees

Sennacherib besieged Jerusalem

            Hezekiah's women are now my sister wives

A palace built
for another, inscribed:

> For my cherished wife
> the goddess of creation
> made more beautiful
> than all others...[80]

I plan

I hear my husband Sennacherib hunts
a man from my homeland—
Tobit, from "good"—this good man
buries Sennacherib's kills
deported dead left rotting in the street
this rebellion of one spun
a hundred chariot wheels

I pray toward where I came from

Sennacherib's two eldest sons—
princes duke it out, embattled
for the crown

I plant an idea

III:

> NAQI'A
> My Lord King Sennacherib,[81]
> you yourself swore by Marduk and Nisrok
> to your maidservant Zakutú:
>
> *Surely our son Esarhaddon*
> *will reign after me, Sennacherib,*
> *and he will sit on my throne*

But now behold, the Prince
Arda-Mussilu consolidates power
to become king, before you
join your fathers
and you my Lord the King
do know it

The eyes of all Assyria are upon you
to tell them who will reign
from the throne of my Lord the King
in Nineveh after him

Melted in my glance[82]
it was done
the crown prince
became *my* son
youngest prince, Esarhaddon

IV:

The rage of elder sons
engulfed their father in the field
courtside, I watched
expectant

My persuasion
to alter succession
fulfilled my promise
efficient

Those sons took a sword
and removed their father's head
roars the foam of his gasping[83]
Sennacherib:
ended

Ancient of bronze dawns
and constellations
I have not forgotten

V:

Now my son Esarhaddon
reigns as king

His son Ashurbanipal will continue
under my guidance as Queen Mother

The roads are safe
from the former king's raids
and my bed also

Fewer bodies
left in the streets

The one who rots
is unnamed he

I put his name
to death

And the Assyrian throne
belongs to me

Epilogue

Inscription on a Concave Zircon–Glass Fragment

Collection ID: MO.1111356

Date: 700–600 BCE

Discovery: Africa: Egypt, 40 km east of the Libyan border near Siwa

Medium: "Etching" in concave zircon-glass fragment (transparent yellow), text appears melted into surface

Dimensions: 17 cm x 17.5 cm x 7 cm

Current Location: Not on view

Language: Neo-Assyrian cuneiform and as yet unknown script, possible translated version of the same text

Provenance:

Assyrian Empire?, circa seventh century BCE. Discovered in Egypt in the twentieth century by local inhabitants from Siwa. Privately purchased on September 17, 1930 in Cairo by Dr. Eleanora Mendez, Allston, Massachusetts (1899–1983); By descent in the Mendez family until 1993; Purchased at auction in 1993 by Marie-Elise Blanc, Geneva, Switzerland; Acquisitioned at auction in 2048 by Museum of the Jinn, Dubai, United Arab Emirates.

Translation from Akkadian (Neo-Assyrian cuneiform) transcription:

Thrown star.

Engulfed.

Still here.

Locked up.

Entombed.

Out west.

[...]

Or am I?

A notation in Spanish accompanies the object, dated 1931, presumed from the original discovery by Dr. Mendez: *El final del mensaje no se ha encontrado.*[84]
2053 CE: United Arab Emirates Media Coverage

THE NATIONAL: "THROWN STAR" SHARD AT MUSEUM OF THE JINN

Since the acquisition of ancient zircon shard originating in Egypt known as the "Thrown Star" fragment (MO.1111356) by Museum of the Jinn, distinguished historians and language experts from around the world have petitioned to be granted an audience with the unprecedented artifact, now housed in Dubai. Discovery of the unique combination of inscriptions in both

Akkadian cuneiform circa seventh century BCE as well as an as yet undeciphered writing system not previously documented generated clamorous appeals from the academy as well as the general public to unveil the object. After more than three years of delays, this month MOJ finally acceded to a small number of select research requests, although the piece remains not on view at the museum...

TIME OUT DUBAI: *YOUR WEEKEND FEATURE—MUSEUM OF THE JINN*

Though "Thrown Star," the hottest Jinn artifact to hit international news in two decades, is still under wraps at Dubai's Museum of the Jinn, there are plenty of other exhibits for the curious, the confounded, and the kids. World-renowned multimedia storytelling exhibits (including holograms!), artifacts, artwork, and a Jinn-themed interactive section feature as the main attractions, while the museum's five! Michelin-star rated café IFRIT and award-winning boutique have everything to quench your appetite for gold-flecked desert-mystery-inspired desserts and a wide variety of souvenirs from luxury items to postcards to commemorate your spirited visit...

[Musuem of the Jinn, متحف الجن Sheikh Zayed Road, Dubai, Sat-Thu 10am-4pm, Dhs40]

KHALEEJ TIMES: *UNCOVERING THE "THRONE STAR"*

In a conference room of Ma'az Tower, fifty floors above the sparkling museum corridors accessible to the public, white gloved with a full complement of state-of-the-art microscopes, lights, and cameras, two scholars pore over the fragment. One, Dr. Sarah T. Toviah of the United Kingdom, internationally-recognized professor of ancient Near East languages, and her associate, R. Azariah...

Endnotes

PART I: CLASH OF CIRCUMSTANCE

1 Echoes of Sophocles' *Antigone* haunt Tobit's lawbreaking gravedigging, "I go to heap dirt upon my brother…" Sophocles, *Antigone*, trans. Robert Whitelaw (Oxford: Oxford University Press, 1906), 3.

2 "Alas, poor Yorick! I knew him, Horatio; a fellow of infinite jest, of most excellent fancy. He hath borne me on his back a thousand times. And now, how abhorred in my imagination it is! My gorge rises at it. Here hung those lips that I have kissed I know not how oft. Where be your gibes now? Your gambols, your songs…?" William Shakespeare, *The Tragedy of Hamlet Prince of Denmark* (New York: Penguin Press, 1998), 125.

3 "…death's dark cloud surrounded us…" Homer, *The Odyssey*, trans. Emily Wilson (New York: W.W. Norton, 2017), 157.

4 "he is already at home and planting ruin for the suitors" Homer, 356.

5   "Es scheinen die alten Weiden so grau" English: The old willows seem so gray. Johann Wolfgang von Goethe, *Goethe: Selected Verse*, trans. David Luke (London: Penguin Books, 1964), 181.

6   Esther 4:14.

7   "…night of her hair…" Hafiz, *Poems from the Divan of Hafiz*, trans. Getrude Lowthian Bell (London: William Heinemann, 1897), 67.

8   "I can show you everything, he said to Gillian Perholt, gripping her elbow, I know things you will never find out for yourself." A. S. Byatt, *The Djinn in the Nightengale's Eye: Five Fairy Stories* (New York: Vintage, 1994), 136.

9   "Hermes fastened on his feet the sandals of everlasting gold on which he flies on breath of air…." Homer, 181.

10 For more detail on Raphael's deceit, see: Geoffrey D. Miller, "Raphael the Liar: Angelic Deceit and Testing in the Book of Tobit," *The Catholic Biblical Quarterly* ٧٤, no. ٢٠١٢) ٣): 492–508.

11 "…a standard and widespread topos within contemporary Jewish thought. Angels do not eat, or at least they do not eat earthly food." Crispin H.T. Fletcher-Louis, *Luke-Acts: Angels, Christology and Soteriology* (Tübingen: Mohr Siebeck, 1997), 64.

12 "…cohorts gleaming in purple and gold…" George Gordon, *The Works of Lord Byron* (London: John Murray, 1842), 467.

13 Marc Van De Mieroop, *Philosophy Before the Greeks: The Pursuit of Truth in Ancient Babylonia* (Princeton: Princeton University Press, 2017), 89.

14 "He has a complete set of Balzac's works, twenty-seven volumes, piled up near his sofa, one of which he threatens to throw at Watkins whenever that exemplary serving-man

appears with his meals." Thomas Bailey Aldrich, *Marjorie Daw and Other Stories* (Boston: Houghton Mifflin, 1901), 2.

15 Elam was a region in what is now southwestern Iran. Robert J. Littman, *Tobit: The Book of Tobit in Codex Sinaiticus* (Leiden: Brill, 2008), 67.

16 "A wife of noble character who can find? She is worth far more than rubies." (NIV) Proverbs 31:10.

17 Polonius: "This above all, to thine own self be true" Shakespeare, 22.

18 Polonius: "The time invites you." Shakespeare, 22.

19 Laertes: "I stay too long. But here my father comes. A double blessing is a double grace;" Shakespeare, 21.

20 Polonius: "I will be brief." Shakespeare, 41.

21 Polonius: "Therefore, since brevity is the soul of wit" Shakespeare, 41.

22 "...endogamy is also a necessary element in Israel's eschatology...The telos of endogamy is thus the ingathering of the exiles." Levine, "Redrawing the Boundaries: A New Look at 'Diaspora as Metaphor: Bodies and Boundaries in the Book of Tobit'," in *A Feminist Companion to Tobit and Judith*, ed. Athalya Brenner-Idan with Helen Efthimiadis-Keith (London: Bloomsbury T&T Clark, 2015), 10.

23 Polonius: "Neither a borrower nor a lender be," Shakespeare, 22.

24 Laertes: "Most humbly do I take my leave…" Shakespeare, 22.

PART II: ROAD TRIP

25 Multiocular O, from Old Church Slavonic, appears in a single phrase in a 15th century book of Psalms, "серафими много⊛читїй (abbreviated мно⊛читїй) 'many-eyed

seraphim'. Michael Everson, "Proposal to revise the glyph of CYRILLIC LETTER MULTIOCULAR O," Privacy & Terms, Google, last modified January 9, 2022, http://www.unicode.org/wg2/docs/n5170-multiocular-o.pdf.

26   Benito Cereno and Chris Sims, "Bonus Goat", *Apocrypals,* podcast audio, July 30, 2018, https://apocrypals.libsyn.com/13-bonus-goat-the-deuterocanonical-book-of-tobit.

27   The Tigris is to the west of Nineveh, and thus away from a destination of Rages, Media. Michael David Coogan, *The New Oxford Annotated Bible with Apocrypha: New Revised Standard Edition* (Oxford: Oxford University Press, 2010), 1377.

28   "Athena's clear bright eyes met his. She said 'Yes, I will tell you everything…'" Homer, 111.

29   "…the historical map generated by this geographical figure is both imaginary and unstable." Amy-Jill Levine, 5.

30   "Are you a friend who visited my father?" Homer, 111.

31   Parasang is an ancient Persian unit of walking distance, roughly 3.5 miles. F.C. Conybeare et al., *The Story of Ahikar,* (London: Cambridge University Press, 1913), 121.

32   There is similarity between the dog Argos in the Odyssey and the dog in Tobit. Joseph A. Fitzmyer, *Tobit* (Berlin: Walter de Gruyter, 2003), 277.

33   Levine, 10.

34   Devren Hobbs, "Revisiting Short Skirt / Long Jacket," last modified October 27, 2016, https://medium.com/@devrenhobbs/revisiting-short-skirt-long-jacket-7d395538a8c9.

35   Though Edna has no verbal contribution to the marriage agreement scene, she is seen to retrieve the marriage documents and serve as a witness, "Edna…may also have actively participated in the signing of her daughter's

marriage contract; the Greek says 'they set their seals to it'..." Beverly Bow, "Edna," in *Women in Scripture: A Dictionary of Named and Unnamed Women in the Hebrew Bible, the Apocryphal/Deuterocanonical Books and New Testament*, ed. Carol L. Meyers, Ross S. Kraemer, Toni Craven (Minneapolis: Houghton Mifflin Harcourt, 2000), 72.

36 Helen: "Do we know who these men are, Menelaus, who have arrived here in our house? Shall I conceal my thoughts or speak? I feel compelled to say, the sight of them amazes me." Homer, 156.

37 Aly A. Barakat, "Iron Deposit and Its Bearing on the Meteorite Impact Event in the Libyan Glass Area Southwestern Egypt," 81st Annual Meeting of The Meteoritical Society (2018): 170. https://www.hou.usra.edu/meetings/metsoc2018/pdf/6006.pdf

38 A nod to the frequently used Biblical phrase ""until this day", i.e. Genesis 19:37, 38; 26:33; 32:33; 35:20; 47:26. See Jeffrey C. Geoghegan, "Until This Day' and the Preexilic Redaction of Deuteronomistic History," *Journal of Biblical Literature* 122, no. 2 (Summer 2003): 204.

39 "Light the fire and roast the meat!" Homer, 353.

40 Fletcher-Louis, 64.

41 "...a man whose white bones may be lying in the rain..." Homer, 110.

42 "Telemachus, sweet light! I was sure I would never see you anymore..." Homer, 387.

43 "He has a goddess as his guide—Athena, a helper many men have prayed to have..." Homer, 178.

44 "...I will send you off with precious gifts..." Homer, 170.

45 "The rabbis...demanded that [a husband] respect his wife and not make her cry." Rabbi Yechlel Eckstein, *How Firm a Foundation* (Boston: Paraclete Press, 1997), 138.

46 "Dawn appeared and touched the sky with roses..." Homer, 220.

47 "The winds have seized him..." Homer, 113.

48 "Stick to the loom and distaff..." Homer, 116.

49 "In the 10th century the great Arab physician Rhazes used gall as an ingredient to treat cataracts, pterygium and leucomas where the blindness was caused by a Vitamin A deficiency." Littman, 109.

50 "[Helen] lifted the most elaborate and largest robe that shone like starlight..." Homer, 353.

51 Daniel 3:8-25.

52 "[Raphael] never speaks with women, and he avoids their company." Levine, 11-12.

53 "There are numerous parallels between Sarah of Genesis and Sarah of *Tobit*, including their beauty, inability to conceive, sexual attention from inappropriate partners..." Levine, 14.

Part IV: Aftereffects

54 The exact location of the Handuri Gate is unknown, likely the southwest corner of the city of Nineveh, on the Tigris River, not far south of the storied Tomb of Jonah. R. Campbell Thompson, "A Selection from the Cuneiform Historical Texts from Nineveh (1927-32)," *Iraq* Vol. 7, No. 2 (Autumn 1940): 93.

55 Jonah 4:5-6.

56 Jonah 2:3-4.

57 Jonah 1:17.

58 Jonah 2:10.

59 Nahum 1:4, 2:8.

60 Jonah 4:4.

61 "...Nineveh...means the city of the fish..." Stephen B. Chapman and Marvin A Sweeney, *The Cambridge Companion to the Hebrew Bible/Old Testament* (New York: Cambridge University Press, 2016), 119.

62 "I suggest that hanging gardens of the deeply sunken bed type first appeared in Sennacherib's Nineveh." Karen Polinger Foster, "The Hanging Gardens of Nineveh" *Iraq 66* (2004): 214.

63 Jonah 3:5-6.

64 "When they believed, we lifted from them the torment of disgrace in this world and allowed them enjoyment for a while" Qur'an: Surah Yunus, 10:98

65 Nahum 1:4-5.

66 In *The Story of Ahikar*, Nadab sets a trap for Ahiqar, forging treacherous letters so that the King wants Ahiqar dead. Conybeare, 140.

67 Ahiqar has no children and adopts Nadab, son of his sister, saying that he will have someone to bury him when he dies. Conybeare, 130.

68 Ahiqar's wife hides him below ground, technically in his own garden. Conybeare, 143.

69 When the executioner comes to Ahiqar's house, Ahiqar reminds him of the time he hid the executioner from King Sennacherib's wrath, saving his life. Conybeare, 142-143.

70 In *The Story of Ahiqar*, Ahiqar admonishes his nephew with a long speech of advice akin to Tobit's admonitions to his son Tobias, and then Nadab dies. Conybeare, 127.

71 Nahum 1:1-3:19.

72 Jonah 3:10.

73 Sarah C. Melville, *The Role of Naqia/Zakutu in Sargonid Politics* (Helsinki: The Neo-Assyrian Text Corpus Project, 1999), 2, 44.

74 Luis Siddall, *The Reign of Adad-nīrārī III* (Leiden: Brill, 2013), 94.

75 Šarratu means "queen" in Akkadian, typically employed not for Assyrian royal women, but *foreign* queens, appropriated here for Naqia, of foreign birth. See Greenfield, "RBT 11 TRRT in the KRT Epic," in *Perspectives on Language and Text Essays and Poems in Honor of Francis I. Andersen's Sixtieth Birthday*, ed. Edgar W. Conrad and Edward G. Newing (Winona Lake: Eisenbrauns, 1987), 37.

76 Zakutú is a translation of Naqi'a, both could mean "pure." Sarah C. Melville, *The Role of Naqi'a/Zakutu in Sargonid Politics* (Helsinki: The Neo-Assyrian Text Corpus Project, 1999), 13-14.

77 Naqi'a is a West Semitic name, Aramaic or Hebrew, not Assyrian. Melville, 14.

78 "When the blue wave rolls nightly on deep Galilee." Gordon, 467.

79 Documented tribute paid by Hezekiah and others in the Annals of Sennacherib: "In addition to the thirty talents of gold and eight hundred talents of silver, gems, antimony, jewels, large carnelians, ivory-inlaid couches, ivory-inlaid chairs, elephant hides, elephant tusks, ebony, boxwood, all kinds of valuable treasures, as well as his daughters, his harem, his male and female musicians, which he had brought after me to Nineveh, my royal city. To pay tribute and to accept servitude, he dispatched his messengers." Antoon Schoors, *The Kingdoms of Israel and Judah in the Eighth and Seventh Centuries B.C.E.*, trans. Michael Lesley (Atlanta: Society of Biblical Literature, 2013), 72-73.

80 Reade, "Was Sennacherib a Feminist?" *La femme dans le Proche-Orient antique. Actes de la 33e Rencontre Assyriologique Internationale* (July 1987): 141.

81 I Kings 1:17–19, adapted for this queen. Some scholars theorize Naqi'a manipulated Sennacherib to alter succession to benefit her son, who appears to be at least fourth in line. Melville, 22.

82 "Hath melted like snow in the glance of the Lord!" Gordon, 467.

83 "And the foam of his gasping lay white on the turf" Gordon, 467.

84 "El fin del manuscrito no se ha encontrado" (The end of the manuscript was not found), last line of the short story, "El Congreso." Jorge Luis Borges, *Cuentos Completos* (New York: Vintage Español, 2019), 468.

Acknowledgments

Thanks to:
    Apocrypals Benito and Chris, scholar-jesters of humorous and courageous insights into all things apocrypha. Mitra and Lauralea, readers and poet-sages. Hillary, writing and mapping guide. Sarah, wayfinder for Akkadian. Joann, co-captain of the starship, for immeasurable gifts of gentle first reader's eyes, expert poetical tailoring, bold opinions, and belly laughs. Sam, Declan, and Aurelia, my muses.

Title Index

T

U

V

X

Y

Z

First Line Index

137

T

W

9 781594 981197